DISCLAIMER:

THE INFORMATION PRESENTED IN THIS BOOK REPRESENTS THE VIEWS OF THE PUBLISHER AS OF THE DATE OF PUBLICATION. THE PUBLISHER RESERVES THE RIGHTS TO ALTER UPDATE THEIR OPINIONS BASED ON NEW CONDITIONS. THIS REPORT IS FOR INFORMATIONAL PURPOSES ONLY. THE AUTHOR AND THE PUBLISHER DO NOT ACCEPT ANY RESPONSIBILITIES FOR ANY LIABILITIES RESULTING FROM THE USE OF THIS INFORMATION. WHILE EVERY ATTEMPT HAS BEEN MADE TO VERIFY THE INFORMATION PROVIDED HERE, THE AUTHOR AND THE PUBLISHER CANNOT ASSUME ANY RESPONSIBILITY FOR ERRORS, INACCURACIES OR OMISSIONS. ANY SIMILARITIES WITH PEOPLE OR FACTS ARE UNINTENTIONAL.

TABLE OF CONTENTS

PERSIAN DESSERTS 5
The Perfect Ending to a Meal...................................5
Chapter 1...8
A TOUCH OF PERSIAN IN YOUR KITCHEN ..8
Chapter 2...11
FRUITS IN DESSERTS..11
    GRAPE MOLASSES.......................................12
    "Grape Sucuk"..12
    PERSIAN GRAPES 15
    FRESH MELON AND PEACH COMPOTE..18
    "Paludah"..18
    DRIED FRUIT AND NUT COMPOTE.........20
    "Kooshaf"..20

Chapter 3...22
PASTRIES, CAKES, COOKIES AND PIES 22
    BOW TIE PASTRY..24
    "Shirini e Papioni"..24
    BAKLAVA 26
    IRANIAN CUPCAKE....................................29
    "Cake Yazdi"..29
    PERSIAN COOKIE..31
    "Kaloocheh"...31
    CREAM PUFF PASTRY 33
    "Noon Khamei"..33
    TIRAMISU 34
    PERSIAN RAISIN COOKIES 39

Chapter 4...41
PUDDINGS AND COLD DESSERTS.................41
    PALOODEH 46
    "Faloudej Shirazi" 46

  BEEF YOGURT 48
  "Khoresht Mast Esfahani" 48
  SHIR BERENJ 50
  ROSE WATER RICE PUDDING 52

Chapter 5 57
Rice Cakes and Sweets 57
  POMEGRANATE SWEET 59
  "Masghati Anar" 59
  DATES AND WALNUTS ROULETTE 61
  "Ranginak Roulette" 61
  ZOOLBIA 63
  BEDOUIN FRESH DATE 65
  "Ragina" 65

Chapter 6 67
Liquid Desserts 67
  MINT SYRUP 67
  "Sharbat e Sekanjebin" 67
  PERSIAN RHUBARB SYRUP 71
  KURDISH TEA 73
  RHUBARB SHERBET DRINK 74
  "Sharbate Rivas" 74

Chapter 7 76
What's On Your Table? 76
  Rose Water 79
  Pomegranates 82

Chapter 8 85
Ending the Meal 85

PERSIAN DESSERTS
The Perfect Ending to a Meal

WHETHER YOU ARE HAVING A 3-COURSE MEAL OR ENJOYING A SIMPLE DINES IN, YOU WILL CHOOSE TO CLOSE IT WITH A LOVELY DESSERT. LIKE EVERY PERFECT BOOK, IT CANNOT BE CONCLUDED IN THE MIDDLE OF AN OPEN PLOT. ALL STORIES DESERVE A PROPER ENDING AND ALL MEALS DESERVE A PERFECT CLOSE—A FINAL SCENE WORTHY OF A STANDING OVATION AND A REMARKABLE CURTAIN CALL, AND THIS IS PROVIDED TO YOU BY A PERFECTLY CHOSEN DESSERT DISH.

DESSERTS MAY BE SERVED IN VARIOUS FORMS. IN THIS BOOK, YOU WILL BE TAUGHT ALL KINDS OF DESSERT DISHES TO SERVE FOR THE RIGHT OCCASION. YOU WILL JOURNEY THROUGH THE PERSIAN CUISINE, IN ITS MOST CHARACTERISTIC FORM, AND THIS BOOK WILL MAKE SURE TO GIVE YOU THE MOST THRILLING RIDE THROUGH DIFFERENT CAKES, PUDDINGS, COOKIES, PASTRIES AND OTHER TASTY TREATS. YOU DO NOT HAVE TO BE AN EXPERT YOU JUST HAVE TO HAVE THE HEART FOR IT. PASSION OFTEN TRUMPS TALENT, EVEN IN COOKING AND IF YOU GET INTO THIS JOURNEY WITH THE RIGHT ATTITUDE, NOTHING WILL GO WRONG.

COOKING IS AN ART EXPRESSION AND WHEN YOU PREPARE A MEAL IT IS LIKE YOU ARE CREATING AN ARTWORK TO BE JUDGED BY YOUR FAMILY, FRIENDS AND LOVED ONES. PREPARING DESSERT DISHES DEMANDS THE MOST ARTISTIC FLAIR OF ALL. IT RELIES NOT JUST ON THE TASTE BUT ALSO COLOR AND PRESENTATION, SO MUCH MORE COMPARED TO SALADS, SOUPS AND OTHER PLATES THAT LEAVE THE KITCHEN. IN THIS BOOK, YOU WILL LEARN ABOUT THE PLAY OF COLORS, AND YOU WILL HOPEFULLY MASTER HOW TO PROPERLY BLEND DIFFERENT FLAVORS, SO THAT YOU CAN SERVE AN AMAZING DISH.

Chapter 1

A Touch of Persian in Your Kitchen

MODERN DAY IRANIAN CUISINE IS KNOWN TO THE WORLD TO HOLD A DEEP HISTORY AND CULTURE. AS A LOCATION EXPERIENCING FOUR SEASONS, ITS CUISINE IS ALSO INFLUENCED THOROUGHLY SO YOU GET TRUE VARIETY—FROM DISHES THAT ARE APT FOR THE TROPICAL SEASONS, TO THOSE THAT WILL BE PERFECT FOR THE COLDER MONTHS.

IN THE CASE OF DESSERT WHICH IS THE FOCUS OF THIS BOOK, YOU WILL COME TO JOURNEY THROUGH THE CLASSICS AND THE KITCHEN INNOVATIONS. AWAY FROM TRADITIONAL KABABS AND HEAVILY SPICED DISHES, YOU WILL EXPLORE A WORLD OF PERSIAN COOKING THAT IS OF A CHARACTER THAT IS TAME AND DELICATE, BUT TRULY EMOTIONAL. THE EMOTIONS THAT DESSERTS EVOKE ARE MEMORABLE AND COLOURFUL. IT IS ABOUT COLOR, SWEETNESS AND ROMANCE. DISHES SPEAK TO THE PERSON THE WAY THE CHEF WISHES TO SPEAK AND DESSERTS ARE AS DAINTY AS THE CUPS AND SAUCERS THEY COME. IN HISTORY
IRANIAN CUISINE IS ONE OF THE MOST INFLUENTIAL CUISINES IN THE WORLD, WITH OVER TWO THOUSAND YEARS OF HISTORY. IT DATES BACK TO THE SIXTH CENTURY B.C. DURING THE TIME OF CYRUS THE GREAT, WHEN HE WAS LEADING THE PARS EMPIRE THAT SCATTERED THROUGH INDIA, GREECE

AND EGYPT. DURING THAT TIME, PERSIANS TRADED WITH THE KINGDOMS OF THE FAR EAST, PASSING THE SILK ROAD, BRINGING FRUITS, RICE AND EGGPLANTS.

DUE TO ITS PROXIMITY, IT HAS DEEP ORIGINS IN THE MESOPOTAMIAN, INDIAN, CENTRAL ASIAN AND ANATOLIAN CUISINE—AND IT HAS ACHIEVED A WIDESPREAD REACH TO VARIOUS NATIONS. FOR INSTANCE, TURKISH CUISINE HAS DEEP ROOTS FROM PERSIAN CUISINE, SO YOU WILL FIND A LOT OF SIMILARITIES BETWEEN THEIR DISHES. IT HAS ALSO ACHIEVED TO INFLUENCE AFGHANISTAN, INDIA, GEORGIA, ARMENIA, AZEBAIJAN, RUSSIA AND THE SOVIET UNION.

AS ALREADY MENTIONED, IT IS DEEPLY ROOTED TO AGRICULTURE SO PERSIAN DISHES ARE MOST POPULAR FOR THE PARTICULAR USE OF HERBS, VEGETABLES AND RICE—AND THEY ARE NOTED AS A HEALTHY CHOICE FOR MEALS. ALSO, AS AN AGRICULTURE-BASED CUISINE, THE USE OF FRUITS IS VERY COMMON. INTRODUCING AN ADVENTURE OF TASTE IS VERY POPULAR IN PERSIAN COOKING. IT IS NOT SURPRISING, THEREFORE, THAT MUCH ATTENTION IS GIVEN TO DESSERTS.

Chapter 2

Fruits in Desserts

THE ABUNDANCE OF FRUITS IN IRAN MAY BE ATTRIBUTED TO ITS CLIMATE. THE CLIMATE IN THE MIDDLE EAST IS VERY CONDUCIVE TO GROWING CROPS, WHICH EXPLAINS THE RICHNESS OF THE AGRICULTURAL INDUSTRY. FRUITS ARE ENJOYED FRESH AND RIPE TO BE COMBINED WITH DESSERTS, BUT THEY MAY ALSO BE USED TO ACCOMPANY MEATS.

IN THE FOLLOWING RECIPES, YOU WILL ENCOUNTER A NUMBER OF FRUITS. FIGS, DATES, APPLES, APRICOTS, PEACHES, SWEET AND SOUR CHERRIES, GRAPES, PEARS, PLUMS, MELONS, POMEGRANATES AND VARIOUS CITRUS FRUITS ARE COMMON IN IRAN AND THEY SHOWCASE PROMINENCE IN VARIOUS DESSERT DISHES.

GRAPE MOLASSES
"Grape Sucuk"

PREPARATION TIME: 15 MINUTES (PLUS COOLING AND SETTING TIME)
SERVING: GOOD FOR 2

INGREDIENTS
3.5 LB SEEDLESS GRAPES
¼ TSP SAFFRON
1 TSP GINGER POWDER
12 OZ WALNUTS
1 CUP SUGAR

INSTRUCTIONS

1. PLACE GRAPES IN A BOWL AND MASH THEM WITH AN ELECTRONIC MASHER OR DO IT BY HAND, IF WITHOUT THE EQUIPMENT AND STRAIN THE GRAPE JUICE ACQUIRED FROM MASHING THE FRUIT
2. COLLECT THE JUICE INTO A POT AND ADD GINGER POWDER, SUGAR AND SAFFRON TO THIS POT, STIRRING WELL AND BRING EVERYTHING TO A BOIL
3. GET 2 CUPS OF THE JUICE AND ADD FLOUR AND STIR UNTIL DISSOLVED WELL THEN ADD THIS TO THE JUICE IN THE POT AND LET IT BOIL UNTIL THICKENED
4. WHEN THICK, ADD WALNUTS AND POUR EVERYTHING IN A DEEP DISH AND LET IT COOL IN ROOM TEMPERATURE OR KEEP IN A REFRIGERATOR FOR A FEW DAYS BEFORE SERVING

ALSO KNOWN AS "GRAPE SUJUK", THIS IS A LOVELY SWEET DISH THAT YOU CAN ENJOY WITH A CUP OF TEA OR COFFEE. THIS PARTICULAR RECIPE TEACHES YOU TO CREATE SQUARES, BUT IT COULD ALSO BE ROLLED IN BAKING PAPER AND SERVED LIKE TAFFY.

PERSIAN GRAPES

PREPARATION: 5 MINUTES (PLUS CHILLING TIME)
SERVING: GOOD FOR 6

INGREDIENTS
1 ½ CUPS SEEDLESS GRAPES
1 OZ VANILLA YOGURT
¼ CUP AND 2 TBSP BROWN SUGAR

INSTRUCTIONS
1. GET SIX CUPS AND DIVIDE THE GRAPES PIECES BETWEEN EACH ONE OF THEM
2. DIVIDE THE YOGURT EVENLY, AS WELL, POURING IT OVER THE GRAPES
3. TO EACH CUP, ADD 1 TBSP OF BROWN SUGAR THEN CHILL IT FOR SEVERAL HOURS

THIS IS A VERY SIMPLE YET TASTY PERSIAN DESSERT THAT YOU CAN SERVE TO CHILDREN. ADJUST THE SWEETNESS IF YOU WANT TO CUT DOWN ON SUGAR, BUT IT IS RATHER HEALTHY. IT IS EASY-TO-DO AND CAN BE DONE WITH THE CHILDREN AND DEPENDING ON WHAT GLASS YOU CHOOSE TO SERVE IT ON, YOU CAN MAKE IT FANCIER.

PERSIAN FRUIT SALAD

PREPARATION: 5 MINUTES
SERVING: GOOD FOR 6
INGREDIENTS
2 ORANGES, CORED AND PEELED
2 APPLES, CORED AND PEELED
2 BANANAS, SLICED
1 CUP DRIED FIGS
2 CUPS PITTED DATES, CHOPPED
1 CUP ALMONDS, CHOPPED
1 CUP ORANGE JUICE

INSTRUCTIONS
1. PLACE THE FRUITS ON THE BOWL
2. POUR ORANGE JUICES
3. GARNISH EVERYTHING WITH ALMONDS AND CHILL, THEN SERVE

THIS FRUIT SALAD RECIPE IS COMMONLY SERVED DURING THE SUMMER. IT IS HEALTHY AND THE FRUITS GIVE THE TABLE MUCH COLOR. FOR THIS PARTICULAR RECIPE, YOU CAN SUBSTITUTE COCONUT FOR ALMONDS, DEPENDING ON THE TASTE YOU ARE GOING FOR. THEY ARE DIFFERENT IN TEXTURE, BUT BOTH WILL BE VERY INTERESTING.

FRESH MELON AND PEACH COMPOTE
"Paludah"

PREPARATION: 15 MINUTES (PLUS CHILLING TIME)
SERVING: GOOD FOR 4 TO 6

INGREDIENTS
2 PEACHES, PEELED AND HALVED
½ CUP SUGAR
½ TSP SALT
1 PERSIAN MELON
3 TBSP LEMON JUICE
2 TBSP ROSE WATER

INSTRUCTIONS
1. CUT THE MELONS AND REMOVE THE SEEDS, THEN USING A SCOOP MAKE AS MANY MELON BALLS AS YOU CAN AND PLACE THEM ALL IN A BOWL
2. TOSS IN SOME SALT
3. ADD THE PEACHES, ROSE WATER AND LEMON JUICE, MIXING EVERYTHING TOGETHER AND REFRIGERATE UNTIL CHILLED

THIS RECIPE IS QUITE SPECIAL AND IS VERY HEALTHY. WHILE IT IS MORE AUTHENTIC TO USE PERSIAN MELONS, IT IS NOT SO BAD TO USE CANTALOUPES. THEY ARE SMALLER SO 2 CANTALOUPES WOULD SUBSTITUTE FOR A MELON. YOU ALSO HAVE AN OPTION TO USE ICE OR YOU CAN SIMPLY CHILL IT FOR LONGER IN THE FREEZER.

DRIED FRUIT AND NUT COMPOTE
"Kooshaf"

PREPARATION: 50 MINUTES (PLUS CHILLING TIME)
SERVING: GOOD FOR 8

INGREDIENTS
½ CUP GRANULATED SUGAR
½ PINE NUTS
1/3 CUP WALNUTS
1/3 PISTACHIO NUTS
1/3 CUP ALMONDS
3 TBSP ORANGE BLOSSOM WATER
1 CUP DRIED APRICOTS
1 CUP SEEDLESS RAISINS

INSTRUCTIONS
1. RINSE THE APRICOTS AND RAISINS UNDER COLD WATER THEN SET THEM ASIDE, STILL SOAKED UNDER WATER
2. GATHER ALL THE DIFFERENT NUTS AND PUT THEM IN THE BOWL. ALLOW EVERYTHING TO SOAK IN BOILING WATER FOR AS MUCH AS 45 MINUTES
3. IN ANOTHER BOWL, COMBINE THE FRUITS, ORANGE BLOSSOM WATER AND SUGAR TOGETHER, MAKING SURE THAT THE SUGAR DISSOLVES WELL
4. RINSE THE NUTS AND ADD THEM TO THE MIXTURE. CHILL FOR A WHILE THEN

SERVE

ALTHOUGH THIS RECIPE CALLS FOR SIMPLY SOAKING THE FRUITS, THERE IS A VERSION OF THIS COMPOTE DISH THAT CALLS FOR THE STEWING OF DRIED FRUITS THAT MAKES EVERYTHING SOFTER AND RATHER TASTIER. FEEL FREE TO STEW IT WHEN YOU TRY IT AT HOME. KOOSHAF IS A COMMON SPECIALTY IN MOST STREET FAIRS, BUT IT IS ALSO FAMOUS IN ORDINARY HOMES, SERVED TO GUESTS.

Chapter 3
Pastries, Cakes, Cookies and Pies

THE MOST FAMOUS DESSERTS ARE PASTRIES, CAKES, COOKIES AND PIES. THEY ARE THE MOST BEAUTIFUL COMPACT CREATIONS AND ARE LOVELY NOT ONLY TO THE EYE BUT IT IS HEAVEN WITH EVERY BITE. THEY ARE DESSERTS ON-THE-GO AND ARE EASILY EATEN EVEN WITHOUT A PLATE, SO THEY ARE GOOD TO BE SERVED AS COCKTAILS.

THE COLLECTION OF PERSIAN DESSERTS IN THIS CATEGORY SHOWCASES VARIETY IN TERMS OF FLAVOUR AND PRESENTATION. ENJOY THE AMAZING JOURNEY AND GIVE YOURSELF A CHANCE TO SHINE WITH YOUR FAMILY AND FRIENDS.

BOW TIE PASTRY
"Shirini e Papioni"

PREPARATION TIME: 30 MINUTES
SERVING: GOOD FOR 4 TO 6

INGREDIENTS
½ LB PUFF PASTRY DOUGH
PASTRY DOUGH
¼ CUP POWDER SUGAR
ALL-PURPOSE FLOUR

INSTRUCTIONS
1. PREHEAT THE OVEN TO 350 DEGREES
2. ON A RECTANGULAR THIN SHEET, ROLL THE DOUGH UNTIL PROPERLY BLENDED
3. CUT THE DOUGH INTO SMALL SIZES (ABOUT 1X2 INCHES IN MEASUREMENT)
4. TWIST THE DOUGH IN THE MIDDLE AND LAY THEM ALL ON A COOKIE SHEET AND BAKE THEM IN PREHEATED OVEN UNTIL GOLDEN
5. LET THEM COOL DOWN AND DUST IT WITH SUGAR POWDER, THEN SHAKE THEM INDIVIDUALLY TO GET RID OF THE EXCESS

WHETHER IT IS PREPARED FOR CHILDREN OR THE KID-AT-HEART, "SHIRINI E PAPIONI" IS A FUN DESSERT OR SNACK TO HAVE. CREATIVELY SHAPED INTO BOWTIE COOKIES,

YOU CAN DRESS THEM FOR A THEMED PARTY OR SIMPLY ENJOY THEM PLAIN. DESSERTS ARE MEANT TO BE FUN AND THIS BOW TIE PASTRY WILL SURELY BE FUN ON YOUR PLATE.

BAKLAVA

PREPARATION TIME: 60 MINUTES
SERVING: GOOD FOR 4 TO 6

INGREDIENTS
¼ CUP SUGAR
1 CUP ALL-PURPOSE FLOUR
1 CINNAMON STICK
1 TSP GROUND CINNAMON
1 TBSP BUTTER, UNSALTED
1 CLOVE
1/3 CUP HONEY
¼ TSP CIDER VINEGAR
½ LEMON, JUICED
1 ½ TSP VEGETABLE OIL
2 OZ PISTACHIOS
1.5 OZ ALMONDS
1.5 OZ WALNUTS
1/8 TSP SALT

INSTRUCTIONS
1. GRIND ALL THE NUTS TOGETHER AND SET ASIDE
2. BOIL 2 CUPS OF WATER THEN POUR AND MIX 1/3 CUP OF WATER IN A BOWL WITH ½ TSP OF VEGETABLE OIL AND CIDER VINEGAR
3. IN A BOWL, MIX THE ALL-PURPOSE FLOUR AND SALT TOGETHER THEN ADD THE OIL AND WATER MIXTURE GRADUALLY, FOLDING IT IN VERY WELL AND ADDING FLOUR SO THAT THE DOUGH IS NOT TOO

STICKY
4. KNEAD THE DOUGH WITH VEGETABLE OIL AND LET IT REST FOR 2 TO 3 HOURS IN A SEALED BOWL. ONCE SET, ADD IN THE GROUND NUTS, CINNAMON GROUND AND CUT DOUGH INTO 6 EQUAL PIECES.
5. GREASE THE PAN AND PREHEAT THE OVEN TO 350 DEGREES
6. ROLL EACH PIECE OF DOUGH OVER THE FLOUR, THEN SLATHER WITH MELTED BUTTER AND PLACE ANOTHER LAYER OF ROLLED FLOUR AND REPEATING THE PREVIOUS STEPS UNTIL YOU ACHIEVE 3 LAYERS OF DOUGH
7. TOP IT WITH THE GROUND NUTS AND BAKE FOR 30 MINUTES OR UNTIL THE DOUGH HAS SEPARATED FROM EACH OTHER, THEN TURN THE TEMPERATURE DOWN TO 300 DEGREES AND COOK A FURTHER 30 MINUTES
8. WHILE BAKING, MIX ¼ HOT WATER, 2 TBSP SUGAR, HONEY, CLOVE, LEMON ZEST AND 1 STICK OF CINNAMON TOGETHER, THEN LET IT SIMMER IN A POT
9. ONCE THE BAKLAVAS ARE DONE, TAKE THEM OUT OF THE OVEN AND POUR THE SYRUP MIXTURE OVER IT AND SERVE IMMEDIATELY

BAKLAVA IS A FAMOUS PASTRY OR DESSERT IN TURKEY AND IRAN. WHILE IT IS NOW AVAILABLE IN A VARIETY OF FLAVOURS, THIS PARTICULAR RECIPE IS BASIC ESPECIALLY

IN TASTE. EVENTUALLY, YOU WILL SEE IT FIT TO EXPLORE MORE DARING INGREDIENTS, SO THAT YOU CAN INTRODUCE DIFFERENT FLAVOURS AND COLOURS TO THE DISH.

IRANIAN CUPCAKE
"Cake Yazdi"

PREPARATION: 30 MINUTES
SERVING: GOOD FOR 4 TO 6

INGREDIENTS
½ CUP SUGAR
1 CUP ALL-PURPOSE FLOUR
½ CUP PLAIN YOGURT
1 TBSP ROSE WATER
2 EGGS
1 TSP GROUND CARDAMOM
1 TSP BAKING POWDER
½ CUP VEGETABLE OIL
SESAME SEEDS

INSTRUCTIONS
1. PREHEAT THE OVEN AT 350 DEGREES
2. BEAT THE EGGS UNTIL THEY ARE STIFF, THEN ADD THE SUGAR AND MIX THEM WELL TOGETHER
3. ADD VEGETABLE OIL TO THE MIXTURE AND BLEND WELL, THEN ADD GROUND CARDAMOM AND ROSE WATER AND STIR WELL

4. FOLD IN BAKING POWDER AND ALL-PURPOSE FLOUR TO THE MIXTURE AND BEAT IT THOROUGHLY
5. POUR THE BATTER INTO MUFFIN/CUPCAKE CUPS, TOP WITH SESAME SEEDS AND BAKE FOR 20 MINUTES

THE PLAY OF FLAVOURS IN THIS CUPCAKE IS TOO DIVERSE. CUPCAKES HAVE AND WILL ALWAYS BE A VERY IMPORTANT PART OF THE DESSERT CULTURE AND WITH THIS RECIPE; THIS MODERN DESSERT IS ABLE TO TAKE YOU BACK IN TIME, MAKING USE OF TRADITIONAL PERSIAN INGREDIENTS.

PERSIAN COOKIE
"Kaloocheh"

PREPARATION: 60 MINUTES
SERVING: GOOD FOR 4 TO 6

INGREDIENTS
¼ TSP SAFFRON
1 OZ BUTTER
3 CUPS FLOUR
1 TBSP COCOA POWDER
1 CUP OIL
¾ CUP SUGAR
½ TSP CARDAMOM

INSTRUCTIONS
1. DISSOLVE SAFFRON IN BOILING WATER FOR ABOUT 30 MINUTES AND SET IT ASIDE
2. IN A POT, LET 1 CUP WATER BOIL AND ADD SUGAR, ROSE WATER AND CARDAMOM. BRING EVERYTHING TO A BOIL THEN LET IT SIMMER FOR 10 MINUTES
3. IN ANOTHER POT, HEAT THE FLOUR UNTIL IT IS DARK THEN SIFT IT IN A COLANDER, THEN POUR IT ALL BACK IN THE POT.
4. ADD BUTTER AND OIL. ADD MORE FLOUR IF IT IS TOO WATERY IN CONSISTENCY.
5. CONTINUE TO HEAT IT IN LOW HEAT UNTIL EVERYTHING HAS COMPLETELY BROWNED

6. MIX THE SAFFRON WATER, GINGER POWDER AND COCOA POWDER AND POUR THEM INTO SEVERAL CUPS
7. ADD THE ROSE WATER MIXTURE PREVIOUSLY PREPARED TO THE CUPS AND MIX THEM PROPERLY
8. DIVIDE THE FLOUR MIXTURE INTO BOWLS AND POUR THE CUP MIXTURES INTO EVERY BOWL AND KNEAD IT UNTIL YOU FORM A SOFT DOUGH
9. SHAPE THEM INTO COOKIES AND BAKE IN A PREHEATED OVEN AT 350 DEGREES UNTIL BROWNED

THIS PERSIAN COOKIE RECIPE IS MADE ALL OVER IRAN AND MAY FEATURE DIFFERENT TASTES FROM REGION TO REGION. KALOOCHEH IS MOST PROMINENT DURING NOROOZ, THE CELEBRATION OF SOUTH OF IRAN AND THEY ARE LOVELY TO BE HAD WITH A CUP OF COFFEE OR TEA. IT MAY ALSO BE ENJOYED WITH ITS CONSTANT PARTNER, MASGHATI, A CRYSTALLINE SOFT DESSERT MADE FROM ROSE WATER.

CREAM PUFF PASTRY
"Noon Khamei"

PREPARATION: 20 MINUTES
SERVING: GOOD FOR 2

INGREDIENTS
1/8 TSP VANILLA POWDER
1 CUP ALL-PURPOSE FLOUR
1 CUP WATER
6 TBSP BUTTER
5 EGGS
WHIPPED CREAM
1/8 TSP SALT

INSTRUCTIONS
1. PREHEAT THE OVEN TO 400 DEGREES
2. IN A POT, COMBINE WATER, BUTTER AND SALT THEN HEAT IT, STIRRING CONSTANTLY
3. SIMMER DOWN AND THEN FOLD IN ALL-PURPOSE FLOUR INTO THE POT, STIRRING WELL AS YOU DO THEN LET IT COOL DOWN
4. ADD THE EGGS, ONE AT A TIME, BEATING THEM WELL
5. ADD THE VANILLA POWDER AND ADD MORE FLOUR TO ACHIEVE PERFECT DOUGHY CONSISTENCY
6. GREASE THE BAKING SHEET AND SCOOP A SPOONFUL OF BATTER ONTO THE BAKING

SHEET AND PUT IT IN THE OVEN. BAKE IT UNTIL GOLDEN
7. ONCE COOLED, FILL THE PUFFS WITH CREAM, JUST RIGHT BEFORE YOU DECIDE TO SERVE IT

CREAM PUFFS ARE LOVELY BECAUSE DESSERT WITH A LOVELY SURPRISE IN THE MIDDLE IS ALWAYS GREAT TO HAVE. THIS PARTICULAR RECIPE FOR NOON KHAMEI (NAN KHAMEI) IS RATHER PLAIN BUT YOU CAN EASILY FLAVOR IT AND TOP IT WITH FRUITS FOR MORE CHARACTER AND COLOR. YOU CAN EITHER INFUSE THE CREAM WITH FRUIT JUICE OR SIMPLY TOP THE PASTRY WITH SOME FRUITS OR SYRUP. IN BAKING, IT IS OFTEN SMART TO START PLAIN SO THAT YOU CAN PERFECT THE BASIC BEFORE YOU START COMPLICATING THINGS.

TIRAMISU

PREPARATION: 15 MINUTES
SERVING: GOOD FOR 4 TO 6

INGREDIENTS
50 LADYFINGERS
6 EGGS
1 CUP WHIPPED CREAM
¾ CUP SUGAR
½ CUP COGNAC
¼ CUP COCOA POWDER
1 ½ CUP ESPRESSO COFFEE
8 OZ MASCARPONE

INSTRUCTIONS
1. SEPARATE THE EGG YOLKS FROM THE EGG WHITES AND SET THEM ASIDE
2. GET THE EGG YOLKS AND BEAT THEM WELL UNTIL CREAMY AND ADD MASCARPONE, MIXING WELL UNTIL BLENDED
3. IN A BOWL, BEAT WHIPPED CREAM UNTIL STIFF AND ADD TO EGG MIXTURE, MIXING WITH A SPATULA
4. IN A SEPARATE BOWL, WHISK THE EGG WHITES UNTIL STIFF AND ADD TO EXISTING MIXTURE
5. MIX THE COGNAC AND THE ESPRESSO
6. DIP THE LADYFINGERS INTO THE LIQUOR MIXTURE AND LAY THEM BEAUTIFULLY ON A BAKING DISH
7. COVER THE LAYER OF LADYFINGERS

WITH HALF OF THE CREAM MIXTURE, COVERING EVERYTHING, THEN DUST IT WITH COCOA POWDER
8. ADD ANOTHER LAYER OF LADYFINGER, THEN CREAM AND COCOA POWDER (AND MORE LAYERS IF YOU HAVE ENOUGH INGREDIENTS TO DO SO)
9. COVER THE BAKING DISH AND REFRIGERATE FOR 24 HOURS

TIRAMISU MAY NOT BE A TRADITIONAL IRANIAN DESSERT BUT IT IS A COMMON DISH THAT IS ENJOYED IN THE REGION AND IS QUITE FAMILIAR TO MANY PEOPLE. IF TO BE SERVED WITH CHILDREN, THE ESPRESSO AND COGNAC CONTENT COULD BE ADJUSTED AND REMOVED. SUBSTITUTE IT WITH COCOA FOR A RICH CHOCOLATE-Y TASTE AND ADD SOME CINNAMON FOR ADDED CHARACTER.

PERSIAN RAISIN COOKIES

PREPARATION: 25 MINUTES
SERVING: GOOD FOR 8 OR MORE

INGREDIENTS
1 CUP BUTTER, UNSALTED
2 CUPS ALL-PURPOSE FLOUR
1 ½ CUPS GRANULATED SUGAR
2 EGGS
½ TSP SAFFRON
1/8 TSP SALT
1 TSP VANILLA EXTRACT
1 ½ CUPS SULTANAS OR RAISINS

INSTRUCTIONS
1. PREHEAT THE OVEN AT 350 DEGREES
2. CREAM THE BUTTER WITH SUGAR UNTIL IT IS FLUFFY
3. BEAT EGGS INTO THE MIXTURE, DOING IT ONE AT A TIME
4. ADD THE SALT, SAFFRON AND VANILLA
5. ADD FLOUR AND BLEND EVERYTHING IN LOW SPEED MIXER OR UNTIL THE FLOUR HAS MOISTENED EVENLY
6. ADD THE RAISINS AND MIX EVERYTHING WELL
7. SCOOP THE DOUGH IN TEASPOONS. ROLL ALL THE BALLS FLAT THEN BAKE THE COOKIES FOR 12 TO 14 MINUTES, UNTIL THE EDGES ARE GOLDEN

THIS IS COOKIE RECIPE IS POPULAR WITH THE CHILDREN BECAUSE IT HAS A LOVELY CHEWY MELT-IN-YOUR-MOUTH CHARACTER TO IT. A GOOD STRATEGY WOULD BE TO REFRIGERATE THE COOKIE DOUGH BEFORE YOU START BAKING SO THAT YOU CAN DEFINITELY MAKE THE COOKIES CHEWY. ALSO, DO NOT MAKE A MISTAKE OF HEATING THE BUTTER. JUST TAKE THE BUTTER OUT EARLIER SO THAT IT MELTS AT ROOM TEMPERATURE. MELTING THE BUTTER IN A PAN OR IN THE MICROWAVE WILL MAKE YOUR BATTER VERY WATERY, YOU WILL NEED TO TOAST THE COOKIES SO IT WOULD COOK.

Chapter 4

Puddings and Cold Desserts

TRADITIONAL IRANIAN ICE CREAM WILL TAKE THE SPOTLIGHT IN THIS SECTION ENTITLED: PUDDINGS AND COLD DESSERTS BECAUSE MANY OF THE ICE CREAM YOU ENJOY TODAY HAVE ROOTS TO PERSIAN ICE CREAM. THEY USUALLY CONTAIN FLAKES OF FROZEN CLOTTED CREAM AND ARE COLOURED AND FLAVOURED BY ROSE WATER AND SAFFRON, BUT LIKE MOST ICE CREAM RECIPES, IT COULD BE DRESSED DIFFERENT WAYS.

THE COLLECTION OF DESSERTS IN THIS CHAPTER, WILL NOT FOCUS ENTIRELY ON PERSIAN ICE CREAM, DESPITE THE INTRODUCTION IT WAS GIVEN. IN FACT, YOU CAN MARVEL AT THE VARIED SELECTION OF COLD DESSERTS IN THIS BOOK.

SAFFRON ICE CREAM

PREPARATION TIME: 30 MINUTES (3 HOURS INCLUDING FREEZING TIME)
SERVING: GOOD FOR 2 TO 4

INGREDIENTS
PISTACHIOS
1 TSP SALEP
¼ CUP ROSE WATER
½ CUP SUGAR
½ LITER MILK
¼ TSP SAFFRON
2 TBSP WHIPPED CREAM

INSTRUCTIONS

1. SOAK ¼ TEASPOON OF SAFFRON IN WATER FOR ABOUT 20 MINUTES AND LET IT BOIL
2. IN A PLATE, SPREAD WHIPPED CREAM AND LET IT SET IN THE FREEZER FOR ABOUT 2 TO 3 HOURS
3. BOIL MILK AND PLACE IT IN A BOWL THEN STIR IN ROSE WATER AND SAFFRON TO THIS MIXTURE. IN ANOTHER BOWL, MIX SALEP AND SUGAR, THEN ADD IT TO THE PREVIOUS MIXTURE, STIRRING WELL
4. LET THIS BOWL SET OVER AN ICE-FILLED BOWL, STIRRING OCCASIONALLY FOR AN HOUR AND ADDING MORE ICE IF NECESSARY
5. PUT THIS BOWL INTO THE FREEZER UNTIL IT IS CREAMY OR SIMPLY POUR CONTENTS INTO A ICE CREAM MAKER MACHINE AND CHURN IT UNTIL PROPERLY BLENDED THEN PLACE IT IN A CONTAINER AND FREEZE FOR AT LEAST THREE HOURS
6. TO SERVE, SPRINKLE LIBERALLY WITH PISTACHIOS AND THE FROZEN WHIPPED CREAM

ICE CREAM IS ALWAYS A POPULAR CHOICE FOR DESSERT ESPECIALLY DURING THE WARM SEASONS OF THE YEAR. THIS SAFFRON ICE CREAM RECIPE SHOWCASES A PERFECT MIX OF FLAVOURS THAT IS HEAVENLY AND AUTHENTICALLY PERSIAN.

THE WHOLE PROCESS IS SIMPLE, BUT THERE

IS SOME WAITING TIME REQUIRED TO LET THE ICE CREAM FREEZE, SO BE PATIENT. NOTE WELL THAT SALEP IS A FLOUR-LIKE SUBSTANCE DERIVED FROM WILD ORCHIDS AND IS COMMON IN DESSERTS AND BEVERAGES. IF YOU CANNOT FIND SALEP IN YOUR AREA, PLAIN COCOA WILL BE A GOOD ALTERNATIVE. IT MAY NOT TASTE AS WELL AS SALEP, BUT IT WILL DO. SOMETIMES, THERE ARE ONLINE STORES THAT CARRY HARD-TO-FIND INGREDIENTS. IF YOUR LOCAL GROCERY DOES NOT CARRY SOME OF THE RECIPES IN THIS BOOK, YOU CAN MAKE AN ONLINE PURCHASE.

PALOODEH
"Faloudej Shirazi"

PREPARATION TIME: 20 MINUTES (PLUS FREEZING TIME)
SERVING: GOOD FOR TWO

INGREDIENTS
1 CUP SUGAR
3 CUPS WATER
¼ CUP ROSE WATER
1 LIME
3.5 OZ RICE NOODLES

INSTRUCTIONS
1. BOIL 2 TO 3 CUPS OF WATER AND SIDE
2. IN A POT, MIX 1 CUP OF WATER AND 1 CUP OF SUGAR AND STIR CONTINUOUSLY UNTIL MIXED WELL THEN TURN OFF HEAT AND LET IT COOL
3. ADD ROSE WATER INTO THE POT AND FREEZE THE MIXTURE
4. WHILE FREEZING THE ROSE WATER MIXTURE, BOIL RICE NOODLES IN A POT AND LET IT SIMMER WHILE COVERED FOR 5 TO 10 MINUTES
5. DRAIN THE NOODLES IN A COLANDER, RINSING WITH WATER AND LET IT COOL
6. ADD THE FROZEN ROSE WATER MIXTURE TO THE RICE NOODLES AND BRING EVERYTHING BACK TO THE FREEZER

7. BEFORE SERVING, ADD A SQUEEZE OF FRESH LIME AND ADD MORE ROSE WATER IF DESIRED

ORIGINALLY CALLED PALLODEH WHICH BASICALLY MEANS "FILTERED", THIS RECIPE HELPS YOU CREATE ONE OF THE POPULAR COLD DESSERTS IN IRAN. IT IS ALSO A PROMINENT FEATURE IN THE NEIGHBOURING COUNTRY, PAKISTAN, AND IS OFTEN SOLD IN MOST ICE CREAM STORES. RICE NOODLES ARE UNIQUELY UTILIZED IN THIS RECIPE. IT PROVIDES TEXTURE AND DEFINITELY MAKES YOUR PLATE SO INTERESTING.

BEEF YOGURT
"Khoresht Mast Esfahani"

PREPARATION: 30 MINUTES
SERVING: GOOD FOR 1

INGREDIENTS
5 TBSP PLAIN YOGURT
¼ LB BEEF NECK
½ CUP EGG YOLK
1 ONION
¼ TSP SAFFRON
½ CUP SUGAR
TURMERIC (A PINCH)

INSTRUCTIONS
1. BOIL 3 TO 4 CUPS OF WATER AND ADD SAFFRON THEN SET ASIDE
2. IN A POT, PLACE THE BEEF AND HALF AN ONION THEN ADD THE BOILING SAFFRON WATER AND SIMMER WITH THE LID COVERED AT LOW HEAT UNTIL THE BEEF IS TENDER
3. ONCE COOKED, MASH THE BEEF IN BLENDER OR SHRED IT BY HAND
4. IN ANOTHER POT, BEAT THE EGG YOLK AND ADD SUGAR
5. ADD THE 5 TBSP OF SUGAR AND CONTINUE TO ADD MORE YOGURT IF THE MIXTURE IS STILL MUCH TOO THICK AND BLEND EVERYTHING TOGETHER UNTIL

YOU ACHIEVE A CREAMY CONSISTENCY.
6. ADD THE BEEF INTO THE POT, STIRRING IT WELL AS YOU DO, THEN REMOVE THE POT FROM THE STOVE AND LET IT COOL IN ROOM TEMPERATURE OR PUT IT INSIDE THE REFRIGERATOR

IT IS ALWAYS FASCINATING TO ENCOUNTER INNOVATIVE DISHES AND THE MERE SOUND OF "BEEF YOGURT" CAN BE QUITE OVERWHELMING TO HEAR ABOUT BUT IT IS A FAMOUS DESSERT DISH IN IRAN. IT IS MADE AND SERVED IN MANY HOMES ALL OVER THE COUNTRY AND IS ALSO POPULAR IN MENUS OF DIFFERENT RESTAURANTS.

IT IS SERVED COLD AND THIS PARTICULAR RECIPE MAY BE DECORATED BY BARBERRIES OR PISTACHIOS FOR MORE FLAVOUR AND COLOUR.

SHIR BERENJ

PREPARATION: 10 MINUTES (PLUS SOAKING TIME)
SERVING: GOOD FOR 2

INGREDIENTS
CHERRY JAM
1 CUP RICE
¼ CUP ROSE WATER
3 CUPS MILK
¼ TSP SALT

INSTRUCTIONS
1. SOAK RICE IN WATER FOR AS LONG AS 8 TO 12 HOURS
2. IN A POT, HEAT THE RICE WITH SALT, UNTIL THE RICE IS TENDER OR THE WATER EVAPORATES
3. ADD MILK AND BRING IT TO A BOIL, STIRRING CONTINUOUSLY
4. AFTER BOILING, ADD THE ROSE WATER, TURN OFF THE HEAT AND KEEP STIRRING

5-WHILE THE JAM IS ONLY AN ADDITIVE TO THE SHIR BERENJ, IT IS AN IMPORTANT COMPONENT. THIS PARTICULAR RECIPE IS NOT SO STRICT IN THE SENSE THAT YOU CAN FREELY CHOOSE WHAT JAM TO USE. HERE, CHERRY JAM WAS CHOSEN BUT YOU CAN EASILY GET A STRAWBERRY, GRAPE OR WHATEVER KIND OF JAM THAT YOU FANCY

THE TASTE OF. THIS SIMPLE RECIPE IS GOOD TO ENJOY WITH COOKIES OR BISCUITS

ROSE WATER RICE PUDDING

PREPARATION: 50 MINUTES
SERVING: GOOD FOR 6

INGREDIENTS
1 CUP PUDDING RICE OR SHORT-GRAIN RICE
¾ CUP FINE SUGAR
2 TBSP CORNSTARCH
2 ½ CUPS WHOLE MILK
3 TBSP WHOLE MILK (FOR MIXING)
FRESH ROSE PETALS
GROUND CINNAMON

INSTRUCTIONS
1. BOIL PUDDING RICE IN A SAUCEPAN AND COOK UNTIL RICE IS TENDER
2. ADD SUGAR AND MILK TO THE RICE THEN LET IT BOIL
3. MIX THE CORNSTARCH WITH THE TABLESPOON OF MILK, CREATING A PASTY CORNSTARCH MIXTURE
4. STIR THE RICE AND ADD THE CORNSTARCH THEN MIX IT WITH THE RICE, STIRRING CONSTANTLY
5. ADD THE ROSE WATER AND BRING EVERYTHING TO A BOIL BUT DO NOT COVER
6. REMOVE EVERYTHING FROM HEAT AND TRANSFER THE RICE INTO DIFFERENT GLASSES AND LET IT COOL OR YOU CAN REFRIGERATE IT
7. DUST IT WITH CINNAMON AND GARNISH

WITH ROSE PETALS

IF YOU ARE FOND OF THE FAMOUS TURKISH DELIGHT, THIS IS A GOOD TWIST TO THE POPULAR DELICACY. IF GARNISHED WELL, IT CAN BE A VERY ROMANTIC DISH WITH ROSE PETALS SCATTERED. PUDDINGS ARE DRAMATIC IN NATURE AND THE PLAY OF COLOR ADDS GREAT EMOTION TO THE DISH. IT IS A PERFECT DESSERT YOU CAN SERVE TO A LOVER OR PARTNER, IF YOU HAVE THE DESIRE TO IMPRESS.

SAFFRON RICE PUDDING "SHOLEH ZARD"

PREPARATION: 2 HOURS
SERVING: GOOD FOR 2

INGREDIENTS
2 QUARTS WATER
PINCH OF SALT
1 TBSP WATER
2 CUPS SUGAR
1 CUP UNCOOKED LONG GRAIN RICE
1 ½ TSP SAFFRON THREADS
8 TBSP BUTTER
6 TBSP ALMONDS, SLIVERED
8 WHOLE ALMONDS, BLANCHED
4 TBSP, UNSALTED PISTACHIOS, CHOPPED
1 TSP GROUND CINNAMON
½ CUP BOTTLED ROSE WATER

INSTRUCTIONS
1. WASH THE RICE, TAKE OUT THE DISCOLOURED GRAINS AND WASH THEM IN A COLANDER
2. IN A BOWL, PLACE THE RICE AND LET IT SOAK IN WATER AND SALT FOR ABOUT 2 HOURS
3. LET 2 QUARTZ OF WATER BOIL AND ADD THE RICE, COOKING IT UNCOVERED FOR 30 MINUTES
4. ADD THE SUGAR, SAFFRON AND BUTTER, THEN ALLOW THE BUTTER TO MELT

UNTIL THE RICE APPEARS YELLOW
5. ADD THE ALMONDS AND PISTACHIOS THEN COOK EVERYTHING FOR 30 MORE MINUTES UNTIL IT IS THICK, THEN ADD ROSE WATER, MIXING IT WELL
6. SERVE THIS IN A BOWL, SPREADING IT USING A SPATULA THEN DUSTING IT WITH CINNAMON AND GARNISHING IT WITH ALMONDS AND PISTACHIOS
7. REFRIGERATE THE PUDDING UNTIL PROPERLY CHILLED

ALTHOUGH IT IS QUITE LABOUR INTENSIVE, THE TRUE FULFILMENT THAT A FINISHED MASTERPIECE BRINGS APART FROM A SATISFIED TUMMY IS A MASSAGED EGO FOR A JOB WELL DONE. MARVEL AT THE INTERESTING USE OF SOME OF THE INGREDIENTS USED IN THIS DISH. A COMBINATION OF TEXTURES AND TASTE, YOU WILL NEVER EXPERIENCE ANYWHERE.

Chapter 5

Rice Cakes and Sweets

WHEN YOU SPEAK OF DESSERTS, SWEETS WILL ALWAYS BE THOUGHT OF AND THERE ARE MANY TYPES OF SWEETS THAT WILL FALL UNDER THIS CATEGORY. RICE IS A PROMINENT FEATURE IN PERSIAN COOKING SO IT IS NOT SURPRISING THAT RICE CAKES SHARE ENOUGH

OF THE SPOTLIGHT ALONG WITH ALL THE OTHER DESSERT DISHES IN THE PERSIAN CUISINE.

RICE CAKES AND SWEETS MAKE AMAZING DESSERTS BECAUSE EVEN A SMALL SERVING IS ENOUGH TO WRAP UP THE MEAL.

POMEGRANATE SWEET
"Masghati Anar"

PREPARATION: 15 MINUTES
SERVING: GOOD FOR 4 TO 6

INGREDIENTS
2 POMEGRANATES
¼ CUP SUGAR
2 TBSP CORNSTARCH
VEGETABLE OIL
1 TBSP BUTTER, UNSALTED

INSTRUCTIONS
1. OPEN THE POMEGRANATES AND SEED THEM, THEN BLEND THE SEEDS IN A MIXER
2. STRAIN ALL THE COLLECTED POMEGRANATE JUICE AND TRANSFER IT IN A POT
3. BRING THE POT TO MEDIUM HEAT AND ADD CORNSTARCH, MIXING WELL FOR ABOUT 10 MINUTES
4. ONCE THE CORNSTARCH MIXTURE IS THICK, ADD BUTTER SUGAR AND POMEGRANATE SEEDS, STIRRING AS YOU DO AND MAKING SURE TO DISSOLVE EVERYTHING COMPLETELY
5. GREASE A PAN LIBERALLY, POUR IN THE MIXTURE AND LET IT COOL
6. CUT THEM INTO CUBES AND SERVE

A DESSERT MOST OFTEN ENJOYED WITH PERSIAN COOKIES OR "KALOOCHEH". MASGHATI ANAR IS A SWEET CRYSTALLINE DESSERT. IT MAY BE MADE WITH POMEGRANATES AS IT IS DONE HERE, BUT IT COULD ALSO BE MADE WITH ROSE WATER. MASGHATI ANAR IS SWEET AND LOVELY. IT IS A SPECTACULAR DESSERT DISH THAT IS MORE THAN JUST PRETTY TO LOOK AT.

DATES AND WALNUTS ROULETTE
"Ranginak Roulette"

PREPARATION: 20 MINUTES (PLUS REFRIGERATION TIME)
SERVING: GOOD FOR 4 TO 6

INGREDIENTS
1 ½ LB DATES
7 TBSP BUTTER
1 TSP CINNAMON POWDER
¼ CUP VEGETABLE OIL
2/3 CUP WALNUTS
¾ CUP ALL-PURPOSE FLOUR

INSTRUCTIONS
1. GRIND THE WALNUTS AND SET THEM ASIDE
2. SEED THE DATES AND MASH THEM THEN SPREAD THEM OVER A PLASTIC OR NON-STICK SHEET
3. GREASE A ROLLING PIN
4. HEAT THE ALL-PURPOSE FLOUR UNTIL IT IS BROWNED, STIRRING CONSTANTLY, THEN ADD BUTTER TO THE PAN
5. ADD THE VEGETABLE OIL AND KEEP STIRRING THEN TURN THE HEAT OFF AND ADD CINNAMON POWDER
6. LET THE BATTER COOL AND THEN SPREAD IT OVER THE DATES

7. HEAT THE WALNUTS FOR A FEW MINUTES AND LAYER THEM OVER THE DATES
8. ROLL EVERYTHING CAREFULLY TO FORM A ROULETTE, APPLYING ENOUGH PRESSURE AS YOU DO SO, THEN PUT EVERYTHING IN THE REFRIGERATOR TO LET IT COOL
9. TO SERVE, CUT THEM VERTICALLY AND TOP THEM WITH SHREDDED COCONUT

WHEN YOU SPEAK OF ROULETTE, YOU ARE IMMEDIATELY TRANSPORTED TO A FINE CASINO, COLOURFUL AND FUN, BUT THIS PARTICULAR ROULETTE IS FUN IN A DIFFERENT WAY ALTOGETHER. A PERFECT ADVENTURE OF FLAVORS AND TASTE, IT SHOWCASES DATES IN THE MOST INTERESTING WAY, EVERY BITE YOU MAKE IS UNFORGETTABLE.

ZOOLBIA

PREPARATION: 30 MINUTES (WITH OVERNIGHT SETTING OF MIXTURE)
SERVING: GOOD FOR 2 TO 4

INGREDIENTS

9 OZ KEFIR CHEESE
9 OZ CORNSTARCH
3 TBSP HONEY
3 TBSP ROSE WATER
¼ CUP ROSE WATER
1 TBSP FLOUR
¼ TSP SAFFRON
½ TSP BAKING SODA
½ TSP CITRIC ACID
VEGETABLE OIL

INSTRUCTIONS

1. TO MAKE THE BATTER, COMBINE KEFIR, CORNSTARCH, 3 TABLESPOONS ROSE WATER AND FLOUR, THEN COVER IT AND ALLOW IT TO REST OVERNIGHT IN WARM ROOM TEMPERATURE
2. IN A BOWL, COMBINE 1/3 CUP WATER, SUGAR, ¼ CUP ROSE WATER, SAFFRON, HONEY AND CITRIC ACID THEN TRANSFER EVERYTHING IN A POT AND HEAT IT IN MEDIUM HEAT, STIRRING CONSTANTLY TO DISSOLVE SUGAR. SET ASIDE AND KEEP WARM

3. ONCE THE BATTER HAS SET, OPEN IT AND ADD WATER AND BAKING SODA, ALLOWING IT LOOSEN
4. HEAT VEGETABLE OIL IN A POT AND LAY AN EGG RING, ABOUT 4-INCHES WIDE THEN WITH A PIPING BAG, SWIRL THE BATTER INTO THE RING
5. ONCE THE BATTER IS FLOATING, REMOVE THE RING AND LET THE ZOOLBIA FRY UNTIL GOLDEN THEN REMOVE FROM PAN AND SOAK IN SYRUP

ZOOLBIA WHICH IS ALSO KNOWN AS JALEBU IS A BEAUTIFUL AND TASTY DESSERT TREAT AND IS FUN ESPECIALLY FOR CHILDREN. KEFIR CHEESE OR YOGURT CHEESE IS A VERY TANGY AND RICHLY FLAVOURED CHEESE THAT IS OF SIMILAR TASTE TO BRIE. IT SHOULD BE EASY TO FIND THIS IN GROCERIES BUT IF YOU ARE HAVING DIFFICULTY, KNOW THAT YOU CAN MAKE KEFIR CHEESE BY STRAINING KEFIR OR YOGURT IN CHEESE CLOTH TO DRY IT.

BEDOUIN FRESH DATE
"Ragina"

PREPARATION: 17 MINUTES
SERVING: GOOD FOR 1

INGREDIENTS
7 FRESH DATES
4 ½ TBSP BUTTER
3 ½ TBSP RICE FLOUR OR ALL PURPOSE FLOUR
2 DASHES OF GROUND CARDAMOM

INSTRUCTIONS
1. UNLESS YOU FIND PITTED DATES, REMOVE THE PITS FROM THE DATES AND ARRANGE THEM BEAUTIFULLY ON A SERVING PLATE
2. MELT BUTTER IN PAN AND STIR FLOUR IN, COOKING OVER MEDIUM HEAT, UNTIL THE FLOUR IS GOLDEN BROWN
3. REMOVED FROM HEAT AND ADD THE CARDAMOM
4. ALLOW THE BUTTER TO COOL BUT WHILE IT IS STILL WARM, POUR EVERYTHING OVER THE DATES

DATES ARE POPULAR IN THE MIDDLE EAST, ESPECIALLY FOR DESSERT DISHES AND THIS

ONE SHOWCASES DATES VERY WELL. THIS IS A VERY FAMOUS PERSIAN SWEET DELICACY AND IT GOES PERFECTLY WITH COFFEE AND TEA. DEPENDING ON THE SIZE OF THE DATES THAT YOU FIND, YOU CAN USE SWEETENED DATES, BUT HAVE BITE OF THEM FIRST. DATES CAN BE VERY SWEET SO DO NOT BE TOO GENEROUS OR YOU WILL JUST OVERWHELM YOUR PALATE.

Chapter 6

Liquid Desserts

YOGURTS ARE ALSO POPULAR AND ARE ENJOYED AS A MEAL ACCOMPANIMENT. OTHER DRINKS THAT JOIN THIS CATEGORY ARE SHERBETS WHICH IN THE VERNACULAR ARE KNOWN AS KHAK AND SHARBAT, ARE BEAUTIFULLY SERVED AS AN ICE CREAM FLOAT THAT MAY OR MAY NOT BE GARNISHED BY SPICES SUCH AS NUTMEG AND CINNAMON.

SOME LIQUID DESSERTS ARE STAPLES IN THE HOT SEASONS AND ARE USUALLY SOLD IN KIOSK IN THE STREETS. THEY MAY BE ENJOYED AS A MEAL ACCOMPANIMENT, AS A STAND ALONE DESSERT OR A REFRESHER ON A HOT DAY.

MINT SYRUP
"Sharbat e Sekanjebin"

PREPARATION TIME: 20 MINUTES
SERVING: GOOD FOR 2 TO 4

INGREDIENTS

GREEN FOOD COLORING
½ MINT LEAVES
2 CUPS SUGAR
3 TSP WHITE VINEGAR

INSTRUCTIONS
1. BOIL 1 CUP OF WATER AND ADD 2 CUPS OF SUGAR INTO THE POT, KEEP BOILING UNTIL YOU ACHIEVE A SYRUPY CONSISTENCY
2. ADD MINT LEAVES AND BOIL FOR ANOTHER 15 MINUTES
3. ADD WHITE VINEGAR AND BOIL FOR LONGER AND LET IT COOL AT ROOM TEMPERATURE
4. REMOVE THE MINT LEAVES AND FILTER THE SYRUP, THEN ADD FOOD COLORING

THIS RECIPE FOR SYRUP MAKES A GOOD TOPPING FOR CAKES, PASTRIES AND COOKIES OR YOU CAN INCORPORATE THEM IN TEA OR OTHER BEVERAGE. THE TASTE OF MINT IS HEAVENLY AND THE SCENT WILL BE SOOTHING AND AMAZING.

PERSIAN LOVE TEA

PREPARATION: 20 MINUTES
SERVING: GOOD FOR 4

INGREDIENTS
2 GREEN CARDAMOM PODS
4 CUPS WATER
½ TEASPOON GROUND SAFFRON THREAD
2 TBSP SUGAR
½ CUP ROSE WATER

INSTRUCTIONS

1. GET A KETTLE AND COMBINE THE SPICES, WATER, SUGAR AND ROSE WATER
2. HEAT IT WELL, STIRRING AS YOU DO, TO DISSOLVE THE SUGAR
3. REDUCE THE HEAT AND COVER THE KETTLE AND LET IT SIMMER FOR 15 MINUTES
4. REMOVE THE CARDAMOM PODS AND THEN SERVE

THIS SPECIAL TEA RECIPE HAS EVERY REASON TO BE AN APHRODISIAC AND IT MAY WELL BE ONE. IT TASTES AND SMELLS LIKE ONE, AND IT LIKE MOST APHRODISIACS, THEY ARE HEAVENLY. FOR THIS PARTICULAR RECIPE, FEEL FREE TO ADD SUGAR AS DESIRED.

PERSIAN RHUBARB SYRUP

PREPARATION: 60 MINUTES
SERVING: GOOD FOR 5

INGREDIENTS
3 LBS RHUBARB, CUT
2 CUPS FRESH LIME JUICE
FRESH MINT SPRIG
4 ½ CUPS SUGAR

INSTRUCTIONS
1. BOIL THE RHUBARBS IN A LARGE PAN WITH ¾ CUPS WATER AND COVER AFTER, TO LET IT SIMMER
2. STRAIN IT AND GATHER THE JUICE THEN PUT THE JUICE BACK TO THE PAN
3. ADD LIME JUICE AND SUGAR AND LET IT SIMMER FOR 30 MINUTES, STIRRING AS YOU DO, UNTIL YOU ACHIEVE A SYRUPY CONSISTENCY
4. STRAIN AND STORE

THIS IS NOT EXACTLY A DESSERT RECIPE BUT IT IS A RECIPE THAT WILL BE A GOOD ADDITION TO MOST DESSERT DISHES ESPECIALLY CAKES. SOME PEOPLE WHO MAKE THIS LOVE TO ADD IT TO GINGER ALE OR SELTZER, BUT IT ALSO AWESOME FOR PLAIN VANILLA ICE CREAM ON A HOT DAY.

YOU CAN ALSO MAKE THIS INTO A DRINK BY SIMPLY POURING ½ INCH OF THE SYRUP INTO A GLASS AND ADDING 4 ICE CUBES, THEN FLAVOURING IT WITH GINGER ALE OR SELTZER.

KURDISH TEA

PREPARATION: 10 MINUTES
SERVING: GOOD FOR 4

INGREDIENTS
4 CUPS WATER
2 TBSP HONEY
6 OMANI DRIED LEMONS

INSTRUCTIONS
1. BREAK THE LEMONS AND AFTER REMOVING THE INTERIORS, SAVE THE DRIED PEELS
2. BOIL THE PEELING WITH HONEY AND WATER FOR ABOUT 5 MINUTES
3. ADD SUGAR, TO TASTE THEN STRAIN BEFORE SERVING IT HOT

FOR THOSE LOOKING FOR A SIMPLE FINISH TO A MEAL, TEA IS OFTEN APPLICABLE AND A KURDISH TEA FOLLOWING THIS RECIPE IS SIMPLE, BUT ELEGANT AND DIVINE.

RHUBARB SHERBET DRINK
"Sharbate Rivas"

PREPARATION: 35 MINUTES
SERVING: GOOD FOR 2

INGREDIENTS
1 LB FRESH RHUBARB, WASHED AND TRIMMED
1 ½ CUPS WATER
2 ½ CUPS SUGAR
3 CUPS WATER
CRUSHED ICE (OR SHAVED ICE)

INSTRUCTIONS
1. BRING TOGETHER 1 CUP OF WATER AND RHUBARB IN A SAUCEPAN AND BRING IT TO A BOIL
2. READ HEAT AND COVER, LETTING THINGS SIMMER FOR ABOUT 20 MINUTES
3. ONCE THE RHUBARB IS SOFT, STRAIN IT A DISCARD THE SOLID PARTS
4. MEASURE THE JUICE AND ADD WATER TO MAKE 2 CUPS THEN RETURN EVERYTHING TO THE PAN
5. ADD SUGAR AND LIT IT BOIL OVER MEDIUM HEAT, STIRRING CONSTANTLY
6. REMOVE THE COVER, INCREASE HEAT AND BRING IT TO A BOIL OR UNTIL IT REACHES 220 DEGREES
7. LET IT COOL AND SERVE SYRUP IN A

TUMBLER THEN STIR IN ½ CUP COLD WATER
8. FILL IT WITH CRUSHED OR SHAVED ICE

    EARLIER IN THIS BOOK, A RHUBARB SYRUP RECIPE WAS GIVEN TO YOU THAT COULD BE ADDED TO DISHES, DRINKS OR ICE CREAM. THIS RHUBARB RECIPE PLAYS WITH THE SAME INGREDIENTS IN SHERBET PLATFORM, SHOWING YOU THE TRUEST VERSATILITY OF PERSIAN COOKING.

Chapter 7

What's On Your Table?

THE MASTERS OF THE KITCHEN ARE THE HOSTS OF THE MEAL. IN THE ANCIENT TIMES, WHEN A HOST INVITES PEOPLE OVER AND SERVES THE FOOD ON THE TABLE, HE DOES NOT EAT WITH THE GUESTS. WHILE EVERYONE IS EATING, HE REMAINS STANDING AND WATCHES EVERYONE AS THEY ENJOY EVERY BITE OF THE FOOD HE PREPARED.

APART FROM THIS, YOU CAN EXPECT PERSIAN DINNERS TO BE TRULY BOUNTIFUL. THE ABUNDANCE OF FOOD SELECTION COULD BE NOTED, TO GIVE GUESTS AN AMAZING FEAST FEATURING THE MANY SPECTACULAR DISHES OF IRAN. AND CHEFS, WHO ARE MAINLY WOMEN, PLAY AN IMPORTANT ROLE IN THE BIRTH AND DEVELOPMENT OF THE CUISINE. THE BEST CHEFS IN IRAN ARE WOMEN BE IT IN A LOWLY HOUSEHOLD OR IN A LUXURIOUS PALACE. THE MEN ARE NOT SPECTACULAR COOKS, BUT THEY ARE AMAZING EATERS AND THEY EXPECT THE WOMEN TO SERVE GOOD MEALS—SO YOU HAVE TO KEEP THIS IN MIND WHEN YOU PREPARE YOUR MEAL.

DIFFERENT INGREDIENTS ARE USED AND INTRODUCED IN THIS BOOK BUT THERE ARE A FEW STAPLE FEATURES OF PERSIAN DESSERTS. THESE DESERVE SOME SPOTLIGHT AND IN THE NEXT PARAGRAPHS, YOU WILL COME TO APPRECIATE SO MUCH MORE ABOUT SAFFRON, ROSE WATER AND OTHER INGREDIENTS— GIVING MORE DEPTH AND MEANING TO YOUR COOKING EXPERIENCE IN THE KITCHEN.

SAFFRON

SAFFRON, DERIVED FROM THE FLOWER CROCUS SATIVUS, IS AN EXPENSIVE SPICE AND ALSO KNOWN AS SAFFRON CROCUS. IT OFTEN OCCURS IN THE WILD WITH TASTE AND ODOR THAT DUE TO THE INHERENT CHEMICALS SAFRANAL AND PICROCROCIN.

ITS BEAUTIFUL COLOR OF RICE GOLDEN YELLOW IS CREDITED TO THE CAROTENOID DYE, CROCIN, AND IT IS HAS GAINED TRUE SIGNIFICANCE IN PERSIAN CUISINE BECAUSE IRAN NOW ACCOUNTS FOR ABOUT 90% OF SAFFRON PRODUCTION IN THE WORLD.

IN HISTORY, SAFFRON HAS ACHIEVED A REMARKABLE STAMP:
IT WAS USED IN THE TREATMENT OF VARIOUS ILLNESSES FOR OVER 4,000 YEARS
IT WAS USED AS A POTENT INGREDIENT FOR

MAGICAL POTIONS AND REMEDIES

IT WAS USED AS A DYE FOR TEXTILES

IT WAS USED IN THE MANUFACTURE OF PERFUMES AND BODY WASHES

IT WAS USED AND MIXED INTO HOT TEAS

IT WAS USED AS A DECORATIVE COMPONENT THAT ONE COULD SCATTER OVER BEDS

IT IS A USEFUL APHRODISIAC AND DRUGGING AGENT

IT WAS POPULARLY INFUSED INTO RICE

IT WAS INCORPORATED TO BATHS

IT WAS USED IN THE CURING OF WOUNDS, ESPECIALLY IN THE WAR ERAS

TODAY, SAFFRON THREADS ARE OFTEN SOAKED IN HOT BOILING WATER TO RELEASE ITS BENEFICIAL COMPONENTS. IT HAS AROMA CLOSE TO THAT OF HONEY AND THE TASTE IS JUST AS SWEET. IT GIVES A LOVELY YELLOW-ORANGE TINGE AND IS A MAIN INGREDIENT IN PERSIAN, TURKISH, EUROPEAN AND ARAB CUISINES.

Rose Water

ROSE WATER, WHICH WAS FIRST INTRODUCED BY THE MUSLIM CULTURE, IS DERIVED FROM ACTUAL ROSE PETALS. IT IS MERELY A BY PRODUCT OF THE PRODUCTION OF ROSE OIL, IN THE MANUFACTURE OF PERFUMES, BUT IT HAS BEEN USED IN COOKING BECAUSE OF THE CHARACTERISTIC FLAVOUR IT PROVIDES TO FOOD.

LIKE SAFFRON, IT ALSO HAS MEDICINAL PURPOSES. AS AN INGREDIENT, IT IS GIVEN ROOM IN MIDDLE EASTERN AND PERSIAN CUISINES, ESPECIALLY IN THE CREATION OF RAAHAT, BAKLAVA AND NOUGAT. WITH ITS CHARACTERISTIC TASTE, IT IS HAS BECOME OF VALUE TO MANY PLACES AND THE FOLLOWING ARE SOME OF THE METHOD YOU CAN CREATE ROSE WATER:

1. CRUSHED PETALS METHOD: THIS IS THE MOST DELICATE OF ALL METHODS
   - PUT HALF OF THE PETALS AWAY, MEANWHILE GRIND THE OTHER HALF (USE A PROCESSOR IF PREFERRED)
   - IN A CERAMIC BOWL, GATHER THE LIQUID COLLECTED FROM THE ROSE PETALS AND LEAVE IT FOR A FEW HOURS
   - ADD THE OTHER PETALS AND COVER

THEM, THEN LET IT STAND FOR 24 HOURS
- AFTER 24 HOURS, TRANSFER EVERYTHING INTO A GLASS OR CERAMIC SAUCEPAN (MAKING SURE NOT TO USE METAL) AND SIMMER OVER LOW HEAT
- REMOVE SAUCEPAN ONCE BUBBLES FORM, STRAIN IT WITH A MUSLIN CLOTH SEVERAL TIMES. YOU CAN ALSO DO THIS WITH A COFFEE FILTER
- TO INFUSE IT, POUR THE LIQUID INTO A JAW AND SEAL IT
- PLACE IT IN AN AREA SO IT RECEIVES A LOT OF SUN TO DRAW OUT THE OIL
- PLACE IT IN THE REFRIGERATOR TO STORE

2. ATTAR METHOD: MAKE SURE TO USE THIS WITHIN THE 6 MONTHS OF MAKING IT
   - RUB THE ATTAR OF ROSE WITH SUGAR
   - ADD MAGNESIUM CARBONATE
   - ADD WATER GRADUALLY AND
   - FILTER EVERYTHING THROUGH PAPER AND POUR IN A CLEAN BOTTLE
   - MAKE SURE TO USE IT WITHIN 6 MONTHS OF MAKING IT

3. FRESH PETALS METHOD: THIS HAS AN EVEN SHORTER LIFE SPAN AS ATTAR
   - IN A SAUCEPAN, LAY ALL THE FRESH PETALS AND POUR WATER OVER IT

- BOIL EVERYTHING FOR ABOUT 15 MINUTES THEN COOL IT
- STRAIN THE MIXTURE AND BOTTLE THE WATER
- REFRIGERATE IT

BARBERRY

BARBERRIES OR BERBERIS IS DERIVED FROM AN EVERGREEN SHRUB THAT OCCURS IN SUCH DIVERSITY OVER EUROPE, AMERICA, AFRICA AND ASIA. THEY ARE USED AS FOOD PLANTS AND THEY GROW IN THE WILD.

THEIR EDIBLE SPECIES PRESENT A SHARP ACIDIC FLAVOUR AND IS VERY RICH VITAMIN C. IN PERSIAN COOKING, BARBERRIES ARE ENJOYED WITH RICE AND IT IS ALSO USED AS A FLAVOURING FOR MEATS. THE FRUITS, WHICH ARE PURPLE AND SWEET, ARE STAPLES FOR JAMS AND INFUSIONS AND TAKE THE SCENE IN PERSIAN DESSERTS.

Pomegranates

THE MOST SIGNIFICANT THING ABOUT POMEGRANATES THAT PEOPLE DO NOT NOTICE MUCH IS THE FACT THAT IT HAS ENDLESS BENEFITS. IT IS A HEAVENLY FRUIT AND IN ANCIENT PERSIA, IT IS VERY IMPORTANT. IT IS RICH IN ANTIOXIDANTS AND VITAMINS; WHILE BEING LOW IN SODIUM AND CHOLESTEROL, AND IS BELIEVED TO COMBAT HEAT DISEASE, CANCERS AND HELPS IN THE MAINTENANCE OF HEALTHY SKIN CONDITION.

POMEGRANATES ARE BELIEVED TO HAVE ORIGINATED IN IRAN. TODAY, IT IS WIDESPREAD IN THE MEDITERRANEAN REGION, AFRICA AND CERTAIN PARTS OF ASIA.

USING POMEGRANATES IN THE KITCHEN CAN GO ANY WAY. HOW IT TASTES USUALLY DEPENDS ON THE RIPENESS OR THE SUBSPECIES YOU HAVE IN YOUR HAND. THEY ARE CUT AND SCORED WITH A KNIFE TO REMOVE THE SEEDS OR THEY ARE PEELED. IT COULD BE FROZEN, FIRST, TO MAKE IT EASIER TO PREPARE.

- POMEGRANATE JUICE CAN EITHER BE SWEET OR SOUR AND IS VERY POPULAR IN PERSIAN, ARMENIAN AND INDIAN CUISINE
- GRENADINE SYRUP WHICH IS VERY

FAMOUS USED TO CONTAIN THICKENED POMEGRANATE JUICE, BUT IT IS NOT COMMON TO FIND SIMILAR COMPOSITIONS OF THIS TODAY
- BECAUSE OF ITS ACIDITY, IT USED TO TAKE THE PLACE OF TOMATOES BEFORE THE RED PLUM GOODNESS ARRIVED IN THE MIDDLE EAST

DATES

THE FRUIT, DATE, IS DERIVED FROM THE DATE PALM. IT IS BELIEVED TO HAVE GROWN ORIGINALLY IN IRAQ, BUT HAS SPREAD TO THE NEIGHBOURING COUNTRIES, SUCH AS IRAN AND HAS MADE IT TO ITS CULTURE AND TRADITION. FRESH DATES ARE CRUNCHY ON THE OUTSIDE, BUT WHEN THEY ARE OPENED, THEY ARE QUITE SOFT.

Chapter 8

Ending the Meal

COOKING, ESPECIALLY WHEN YOU DO IT FOR THE PEOPLE YOU CARE ABOUT, IS SOMETHING VERY SPECIAL. COOKING A MEAL CAN BE VERY LABORIOUS AND WITH THE OPTION TO ORDER AND BUY READY-MADE FOOD, IT IS TRULY IMPRESSIVE WHEN ONE MAKES THE DECISION TO IMPRESS WITH A HOME-COOKED MEAL.

PERSIAN COOKING AND PREPARING PERSIAN DESSERTS, MOST SPECIFICALLY, IS A WHOLE NEW EXPERIENCE ALTOGETHER. THIS IS ONE JOURNEY WORTH TAKING BECAUSE OF THE FOLLOWING REASONS:

1. IT IS HEALTHY: AS YOU HAVE PROBABLY DISCOVERED FROM THE INGREDIENTS USED IN THE CREATION OF MOST PERSIAN RECIPES, IT IS ALL ABOUT USING NATURALLY OCCURRING FOOD SUBSTANCES. PROCESSED FOODS ARE RICH IN UNHEALTHY COMPONENTS AND TOXIC CHEMICALS, SO VEERING AWAY FROM THEM WILL BE MORE VALUABLE.

2. EASY-TO-MAKE: MUCH OF RECIPES INCLUDED HERE COULD BE COMPLETED IN LESS THAN AN HOUR. FOR STAY-AT-HOME OR WORKING MOTHERS WHO ARE EXPECTED TO TEND TO A WHOLE FAMILY, IT IS A GOOD THING FOR THEM TO BE ABLE TO FEED EVERYONE WITH SOMETHING THAT DID NOT TAKE MUCH OF THEIR TIME.
3. AMAZING TASTE AND FLAVOUR: WITH THE UNIQUE INGREDIENTS, PERSIAN CUISINE TRULY SHOWCASES FLAVOUR IN THE MOST INTERESTING WAY. THE COLOURS THAT SAFFRON, ROSE WATER AND ALL THE OTHER INGREDIENTS PROVIDE ADD TO THE CREATION OF AN AMAZINGLY POSITIVE EXPERIENCE.
4. DEEP HISTORY: MUCH OF THE TRADITIONAL DISHES SHARED TO YOU IN THIS BOOK HAVE ROOTS DEEP INTO THE CULTURE OF IRAN. MORE THAN JUST EXPERIENCING THE TASTE, WHEN YOU BITE INTO A SPOONFUL, YOU ARE TAKING IN A RICH CULTURE.

PERSIAN DESSERTS LIKE ALL OTHER DISHES IN THE CUISINE WILL BE A TRUE EXPERIENCE FOR YOU. THIS BOOK AIMS TO PROVIDE YOU WITH A GREAT ADVENTURE. HOPEFULLY, THE EXPERIENCE WAS A GOOD ONE.

www.ingramcontent.com/pod-product-compliance
Lightning Source LLC
LaVergne TN
LVHW020419070526
838199LV00055B/3664